On the Threshold of Hope Workbook

Opening the door to healing for survivors of sexual abuse

Diane Mandt Langberg, Ph.D. with Sallie Culbreth, M.S.

Copyright © 2014 by Diane Mandt Langberg, Ph.D. with Sallie Culbreth, M.S.

On the Threshold of Hope Workbook
Opening the door to healing for survivors of sexual abuse
by Diane Mandt Langberg, Ph.D. with Sallie Culbreth, M.S.

Printed in the United States of America

ISBN 9781628716078

All rights reserved solely by the author. The author guarantees all contents are original and do not infringe upon the legal rights of any other person or work. No part of this book may be reproduced in any form without the permission of the author. The views expressed in this book are not necessarily those of the publisher.

Unless otherwise indicated, Bible quotations are taken from New International Version. Copyright © 1973 by Biblica, Inc.

www.xulonpress.com

PART ONE – APPROACHING THE SUBJECT OF SEXUAL ABUSE
Chapter 1-5 (pp. 5-29)

Chapter One–*Getting Started*

Read Chapter One (pp. 5-8) and respond to the following questions, statements or projects:

1. While you read this book, you will come across many voices (p. 6). There are four specific voices that you can expect to hear from:

    - The author's voice (Diane Langberg)
    - Fellow survivor's voices
    - Your own voice
    - The voice of the Redeemer

2. Of these four voices, which ones do you need to hear and why?

3. As you think about what you might hear from these voices, do you have any fears? Explain:

4. Jesus is described as a "Man of Sorrows" (p. 7). How do you think the sorrows that He experienced can help you through your own sorrows?

5. How does the following statement make you feel? "You can be assured that your darkness and suffering are REAL (p. 7)."

6. There is a way out of darkness. Stop for a minute and close your eyes (if you feel comfortable doing so). Imagine that you have been stuck in a very dark room. This room has no windows, no light, no fresh air, the food has spoiled and the water is dirty. You have been there for a long, long time. Now open you eyes and imagine that you have just walked out of that room into a beautiful mountain meadow with warm sunshine, fields of colorful flowers, crisp mountain air, good food and fresh water.

    - Describe how you think you will feel the moment you step through that door:

    - What do you think the meadow will smell like?

- What do you think your body will feel?

- What emotions do you think you will experience?

- Your description of this experience is a description of what **hope** feels like. It is the contrast of standing in beautiful light against the experience of being in darkness and fear for a long time.

7. Look up Hebrews 11:1 and write that verse here:

8. Write a prayer to Jesus and tell Him what you hope for as you face the darkness of your abuse:

Chapter Two–*On the Threshold*

Read Chapter Two (pp. 9-12) and respond to the following questions, statements or projects:

1. Read Judges 19 in the Bible. Are you surprised that this story is in the Bible? Explain:

2. Why do you think God included this story in the Bible?

3. Listed below is a checklist of events from this Bible story. Place a check mark next to the phrases about this story that describe experiences that are like your abuse:

    ☐   The victim's home was supposed to be a place of rest and safety, but was not.

    ☐   The victim's parents knew something was wrong, but did not give protection from unsafe people.

    ☐   The victim was used like a spouse, but was not loved and valued like a spouse is supposed to be.

    ☐   Instead of being protected, the victim was treated as a disposable and meaningless person.

- ☐ The victim was sacrificed, while "decent" people kept up appearances of being righteous and untouched.

  Other people were valued as more important than the victim.

- ☐ Other people were more concerned with their own needs than the needs and safety of the victim.

- ☐ A threat was made to put another innocent child in the same abusive situation.

- ☐ The victim was deliberately placed in an abusive situation by people who should have provided protection.

- ☐ "Religious" people were part of the abuse.

- ☐ Since the victim had already sinned sexually, people thought that it did not matter what happened.

- ☐ The victim was gang raped.

- ☐ The victim was beaten.

- ☐ The victim thought the night would never end.

- ☐ The victim struggled to get to a place of safety, but it was still not a safe place.

- ☐ The only place the victim had to go for help was back to the people that were part of the set up and betrayal in the first place.

- ☐ The victim had no hope.

- ☐ People looked at the evidence of the abuse, and coldly told the victim to "get up," even though that was not possible.

- ☐ The victim was not truly loved.

- ☐ The victim was never safe.

- ☐ Once the abuse occurred and the evidence could not be covered up, the victim's people acted as if they were outraged, even though they were part of the abuse.

- ☐ These are other things I identify with in this story:

4. A "threshold" is a frame that holds a door in place. Imagine that you have reached out and touched a place of real help and real hope–that you have crossed that threshold. In what ways do you have more hope than the victim in Judges 19? Explain:

5. The "hope" that you are promised comes from placing the painful memories and damage from your abuse into the hands of our Redeemer, Jesus. He is a Redeemer who has also been abused. He opened the door for you after He rose from His own abuse. He is offering you the chance to walk across a *new* threshold, into a *new* place, where healing is possible. Write a prayer to Jesus about the hope He offers to you right now:

Chapter Three–*How to Care for Yourself As You Read*

Read Chapter Three (pp. 13-16) and respond to the following questions, statements or projects:

1. Identify some possible reasons that you are drawn to read this book:

    - ☐ There may be hope for me
    - ☐ I may be understood
    - ☐ I might get help
    - ☐ Maybe there is a way out for me
    - ☐ Other reasons that I am drawn to read this book are:

2. Identify some possible reasons that you may be afraid to read this book:

    - ☐ I feel afraid
    - ☐ Hope is dangerous for me because it has been crushed so many times before
    - ☐ I don't know if I have the energy to do this
    - ☐ I am worried that I will fall apart

3. Will you make an effort to take care of yourself while you work through this book?

    - ☐ Yes
    - ☐ No
    - ☐ Not Sure

4. Write down or check off some ways that you will commit to take care of yourself while you read this book?
    - I will usually read this book at: _____ o'clock ☐ a.m.   ☐ p.m.
    - I will usually read this book: ☐ inside   ☐ outside
    - I will read this book in a place that feels safe to me. That place is:
    - I will not read this book all at once. I will not read more than (how many?)____ chapters at one time.
    - I give myself permission to stop when I have had enough. The signals that I will pay attention to, that will let me know it is time to stop reading include:
        - ☐ Feeling overwhelmed
        - ☐ Feeling afraid
        - ☐ Feeling very tired
        - ☐ Feeling pressured to finish
        - ☐ Other signals that let me know it is time to stop include:

    - When I have a feeling or memory while I read this book, I will put the book down and express what I feel or remember:
        - ☐ By writing in a notebook
        - ☐ By writing in a journal
        - ☐ By drawing in a sketch journal
        - ☐ By making an audio recording of my feelings or memories

    - I will be honest and express my:

        - ☐ Feelings
        - ☐ Thoughts
        - ☐ Questions
        - ☐ Memories
        - ☐ Others things I will express:

- These are the names of safe people that I am in a good relationship with:

- I (check one) ☐ will   ☐ will not let them know that I am working on this book.

- These are ways that I will let my safe people know that they can help me:

- I give myself permission to tell these safe people that I do NOT want to talk about this process, if and when I do not want to discuss this. Even if they ARE safe people, I will not allow myself to be pressured to feel or think the way they think or tell me I should.
    ☐ I will try   ☐ I cannot do this   ☐ I am not sure

- These are ways that I will take care of myself while I am working on this book:
    - ☐ Walk, run, bicycle, or swim regularly each week
    - ☐ Attend an exercise class or aerobic workout in a gym or health club regularly each week
    - ☐ Work out with weights several times a week
    - ☐ Listen to music or play a musical instrument
    - ☐ Read something light that has nothing to do with abuse or problems

- ☐ Go to a movie or rent a DVD
- ☐ Draw, paint, sculpt, etc.
- ☐ Dance
- ☐ Creative writing
- ☐ Gardening
- ☐ Crafts or woodworking projects
- ☐ Fish or hunt
- ☐ Other physical or creative activities that will help me take care of myself:

- These are things that I will NOT do while working on this book:
  - ☐ Illegal drugs
  - ☐ Abuse prescription or over-the-counter medications
  - ☐ Abuse alcohol
  - ☐ Abuse my body by self-injury (cutting, burning, etc.)
  - ☐ Binge on food
  - ☐ Purge food through forced vomiting or abuse laxatives
  - ☐ Starve myself
  - ☐ Abuse myself or others with sex
  - ☐ Hurt other people (physically, emotionally, verbally, or spiritually)
  - ☐ View sexually explicit or violent movies, programs, magazines or books
  - ☐ Other things that I will NOT do that could hurt me at this time are:

- I realize that I will probably feel pain at some point in this process. I will make a commitment to myself that I will not run from it, minimize it or ignore it.
  ☐ Yes   ☐ No   ☐ I'm not sure

On the Threshold of Hope Workbook

- Read Isaiah 9:2 and write the verse, word for word:

- Remind yourself of this:

                            That was THEN
                            This is NOW

(You might want to write this out and post it somewhere to remind you of truth)

Chapter Four–*You are a Survivor*

Read Chapter Four (pp. 17-21) and respond to the following questions, statements or projects:

1. A "survivor" is someone who has lived "above or beyond." Someone who has "endured life changing and life shattering events" (p. 17). Do you see yourself as a "survivor?" Explain:

2. How has your world been altered by the abuse you suffered?

3. What characteristics have developed in you as a result of your struggle to survive?

4. What has kept you going when you wanted to quit?

5. Write your response to the following statement: "The fact that you are a survivor is worthy of commendation . . . Hold your head up" (p. 20).

6. Does facing your abuse, confronting the lies and developing strategies for living, seem impossible for you at this time? Explain:

7. You have demonstrated you are a very resourceful person, just because you have survived your abuse. You have used your God-given abilities to endure. Complete the following sentences:
    - I am brave because:

    - I am strong because:

    - I am creative because:

Chapter Five–*One Survivor's Story*

Read Chapter Five (pp. 23-29) and respond to the following questions, statements or projects:

1. If you were friends with Tanya (Tamar) and you heard her story, what would you say to give her hope? Write a letter to Tanya to help her face the pain of sexual abuse.

Dear Tanya,

2. If you had the chance to write a letter to Aaron (Amnon), what would you say to him?

Dear Aaron,

3. If you had an opportunity to write a letter to David, what would you say to him?

Dear David,

PART TWO–DEALING WITH THE ABUSE
Chapter 6-12 (pp. 33-81)

Chapter Six–*Telling Your Story*

Read Chapter Six (pp. 33-37) and respond to the following questions, statements or projects:

1. Place a check mark next to reasons that telling your story is an important exercise:

    ☐ I am beginning to develop new patterns in my life. Telling my story exposes the truth about what happened to me and allows me to begin the process of moving on.

    ☐ I am learning to hear my own voice (the voice that was silenced by abuse).

    ☐ I needed to give witness to the truth.

    ☐ I needed to recognize the conflicts that telling the truth might create in me (called ambivalence).

    ☐ I am no longer willing to tolerate the destructive consequences of abuse and its secrets in my life.

2. Do you need to write your story?

    ☐ Yes   ☐ No   ☐ Not Sure

If so, be sure to do so, now. The truth often comes to you in small pieces and at different times. With each new piece of the puzzle, it is important for you to give witness to it.

3. Abuse damaged your life. In an attempt to survive, you have learned to lie, distort, and deceive (p. 36). On a separate piece of paper, draw a picture that represents the way your life has been damaged by abuse. If you are not comfortable with drawing, then make a collage from magazine pictures and words; write a poem; or write words from a song that expresses how your life has been damaged.

4. God created you for a noble and holy purpose. You need to understand that you are a created in the image of God (p. 37). On a second sheet of paper, draw a picture that represents what God can do in your life. Again, if you are not comfortable with drawing, then make a collage from magazine pictures and words; write a poem; or write words from a song that expresses what God can do in your life.

Chapter Seven–*What Happens After You Tell Your Story*

Read Chapter Seven (pp. 39-42) and respond to the following questions, statements or projects:

1. What did you feel after you wrote your story?

2. How do you feel about yourself since you wrote your story?

3. How do you feel about your abuser(s) since you wrote your story?

4. What are you afraid will happen since you wrote your story?

5. Do you feel relieved and afraid at the same time? Explain:

6. Have you taken care of yourself the way you said you would? Explain:

7. Separate the different voices in your life:
    - What is YOUR voice saying?

    - What is your abuser's voice saying?

    - What is Jesus' voice saying?

Chapter Eight–*Understanding Some Terminology*

Read Chapter Eight (pp. 43-50) and respond to the following questions, statements or projects:

1.   Please fill in the blanks:

   - Sexual abuse occurs when a person is sexually exploited by an older or more _____ person for the satisfaction of the abuser's needs (p. 43).
   - The range of sexual abuse includes three areas. Please list these three areas (p. 44):

   1.
   2.
   3.

2.   Definition of terms:

   - Trigger–anything that reminds _____ of the abuse (p. 46).
   - Flashback–a kind of memory that is so powerful that it _____ as if the present has faded away and you are actually back in the time and place of the abuse (p. 47).
   - Nightmares–many _____ of sexual abuse have repeated _____ nightmares (p. 49).
   - Dissociation–a mental and emotional way of _____ oneself from the hurtful and dangerous present (p. 49).

27

Chapter Nine–*Dealing with Trauma*

Read Chapter Nine (pp. 51-57) and respond to the following questions, statements or projects:

1. Sexual abuse is traumatic and leaves many survivors with Post-Traumatic Stress Disorder (PTSD). Please look at the symptoms of PTSD listed below and identify which, if any, of these you have experienced for at least one month (p. 52):

    - Were you exposed to a traumatic event (sexual abuse), that involved actual or threatened death or injury, during which you experienced panic, horror, or helplessness?
        ☐ Yes   ☐ No   ☐ Not Sure

    - Have you re-experienced the trauma in dreams, flashbacks, intrusive memories, or anxiety in situations that remind you of the events?
        ☐ Yes   ☐ No   ☐ Not Sure

    - Are your emotions numb or have you experienced a lack of interest in or avoidance of others and the world?
        ☐ Yes   ☐ No   ☐ Not Sure

    - Have you experienced symptoms like insomnia, irritability, anger outbursts, and difficulty concentrating?
        ☐ Yes   ☐ No   ☐ Not Sure

    - Do you think you qualify as a sufferer of PTSD? Explain:
        ☐ Yes   ☐ No   ☐ Not Sure

2. Our word trauma comes from the Greek word for "wound" (p. 53). Can you identify the wounds that you have from your sexual abuse? Explain:

3. Since God is a God of truth, why do you think it is important to speak the truth about your abuse in order to find healing from it?

4. Ask God to expose what is true about you, the abuse, and the wounds caused by the abuse:

Chapter Ten–*Childhood Abuse*

Read Chapter Ten (pp. 59-65) and respond to the following questions, statements or projects:

1. When you hear the word "child" what do you think of?

2. If you were responsible for taking care of a child, what kind of a person would you need to be in order to provide for him or her?

3. What happens to a child or young person who is told, year after year, that evil is good or that abuse is love?

4. What does God say about people who teach children lies? (Isaiah 5:18-23)

On the Threshold of Hope Workbook

5. What did you learn about relationships from your abuser(s) that was not the truth? (Examples of what other survivors learned is on page 61)

6. What happens to a child or young person whose body is used for sex and who is told that the shame and guilt are entirely his or hers?

7. When you were a child or young person, what did you learn about your abilities, self-confidence, creativity and initiative from your abuser(s)?

8. Approximately how old were you when the abuse started?

9. Think about a child who is the age that you were when the abuse started. How does this child act? What does this child know how to do? What does this child need? Write down some of your ideas and observations:

10. Survivors think back on their abuse with adult minds. Can you identify ways that you have judged yourself harshly because you are looking at YOU, the child, through the eyes of YOU, the adult? Explain:

11. How does Jesus see children (Matthew 18:1-6)?

Chapter Eleven–*What Did You Learn from Your Family?*

Read Chapter Eleven (pp. 67-72) and respond to the following questions, statements or projects:

1. What are the two general categories of families? (p. 68)

    - _____ which is characterized by respect, concern, teaching, nurturing and reasonable expectations.

    - _____ which is characterized by no respect, unreasonable expectations, criticism and rejection.

2. Which of these categories best describes the family you grew up in?

3. It is important to identify what lessons your family taught you. Take a few minutes and answer these questions:

    - What were the dominant messages that your family gave to you? (p. 72 gives some examples of destructive messages.) Can you identify other messages, as well as these?

    - What were your family's spoken and unspoken rules?

- What patterns are you repeating in your life now?

- What family rules are you afraid to break?

4. What are your thoughts about the following statement: "Until you state what you know, you cannot find out what is a lie and what is the truth. And as long as the lies remain hidden, they will exert a powerful influence over your life." (p. 72) Explain:

Chapter Twelve–*A Look Behind the Scenes*

Read Chapter Twelve (pp. 73-81) and respond to the following questions, statements or projects:

1. Behind all that sexual abuse appears to be, evil is at the heart of it (p. 75). Why do you think it is so important to understand the *evil* behind the scenes of sexual abuse? Explain:

2. Can you identify the rubbish of the enemy in your life as you face the aftereffects of sexual abuse (p. 78)? Explain:

3. The core issue of this battle is TRUTH (p. 78). When you face this battle, what happens if you pretend, minimize or deny the truth? Explain:

4. As you reflect on your abuse and the aftereffects of it, what have you held God responsible for that is really the work of Satan in your life? Explain:

5. Do you understand that this battle is about more than how you feel, or what you have experienced?

6. How are you going to do battle with the powers of darkness and the spiritual forces of evil as you work through the aftereffects of evil? (p. 79-80 gives you some ideas)

7. As much as you need people to pray for you, you need a Champion to see you through this battle, even more. Write a prayer to Jesus about why you need Him to fight this battle:

PART THREE–WHAT WAS DAMAGED IN THE ABUSE?
Chapter 13-17 (pp. 85-135)

<u>Chapter Thirteen–*Abuse Damaged Your Body*</u>

Read Chapter Thirteen (pp. 85-98) and respond to the following questions, statements or projects:

1. What does it mean for you to live in your body? Explain:

2. What happens to children and young people who grow up having other people use their bodies? Explain:

3. When you think about your own body, place a check mark next to the lies that you have believed (p. 88):
    - ☐ I have not thought of my body as my own
    - ☐ I have not believed that I should take good care of my body
    - ☐ I have not felt that I had a choice about what happens to my body
    - ☐ I have developed an attitude of endurance–just trying to survive whatever is happening to my body, hoping to outlast the pain and/or pressure
    - ☐ I have felt disconnected from my own body

4. The feelings of shame that come from sexual abuse can make survivors want to hide (pp. 89-90). How do you hide from your own body? Explain:

5. Sexual abuse survivors often feel as if their own bodies betrayed them. Place a check mark next to the phrases that describe how you feel your body betrayed you:

    ☐ It feels like my body invited the abuse
    ☐ It feels like my body seduced others without my permission
    ☐ It feels like my body was somehow labeled to allow or give permission for it to be abused
    ☐ I am afraid that my body wanted the abuse and I did not know it
    ☐ It feels like my body was unfaithful to me, as a person and as its owner
    ☐ My sense of how my body betrayed me is huge, because I felt some kind of pleasure during the abuse
    ☐ My body longed for touch and affection and I have confused those longings with being abused
    ☐ My body feels like my ultimate enemy

6. Think about the following lies regarding your body, and write down your response to each lie:

    ☐ Lie #1–I am only a body and nothing else (p. 93). This lie means that my value is determined by the way I look. Explain how this lie has affected the way you live:

☐ Lie #2–My body is my enemy (p. 93). This lie means that my body is worthy of punishment. These are the ways I have punished my body:

☐ Lie #3–My body is worthless trash (p. 93). This lie means that my body is not worth taking care of. These are the ways I have not taken care of my body:

☐ Lie #4–My gender is my problem (p. 93). These are the reasons I believe I was abused because of my gender:

7. Think about the following truths regarding your body, and write down your response to each truth:

☐ Truth #1–God made my body and said it was good (p. 94). Complete this sentence: I am "fearfully and wonderfully made" (Psalm 139:13-14) because ...

☐ Truth #2–God chose to live in a human body (p. 95). What can you give yourself permission to feel about your own body since you learned that Jesus chose to live in a human body, too? Explain:

☐ Truth #3–God is willing to live in your body (p. 95). God only lives in your body when you invite Jesus Christ into your life. In what ways, as a follower of Jesus Christ, can you honor God with your body? Explain:

8. Abuse involves evil thoughts, immorality, theft and false testimony (p. 96). "The truth is that the things that came out of the heart of your abuser were the things that made him or her unclean. The abuse did not come from you, and it *does not* make you dirty." What was revealed about the hearts of those who abused you? Explain:

9. What is revealed about your heart when you think about the way you have treated your body? Explain:

10. Do you want to learn a new way, a redeemed way, to live in and with your body? Explain:

11. Jesus Christ died to redeem your heart. This gives you the chance to make some decisions about how you will treat your body. Please place a check next to the changes you want to make because Jesus died to redeem your heart:

- ☐ I want a redeemed heart that does not despise my body
- ☐ I want a redeemed heart that does not destroy my body
- ☐ I want a redeemed heart that does not ignore my body
- ☐ I want to pursue a right relationship with my body
- ☐ I am willing to pursue this right relationship with my body, even if it takes years and hard work
- ☐ I understand that I was bought with the price of God's Son, Jesus Christ
- ☐ I am willing to spend a lifetime learning how to glorify God with my body because of God's love

Chapter Fourteen–*Abuse Damaged Your Emotions*

Read Chapter Fourteen (pp. 99-110) and respond to the following questions, statements or projects:

1. The four emotions most affected by abuse are fear, guilt/shame, anger and grief (p. 99). When you were traumatized, and experienced helplessness, fear became a way of life (p. 100). It is important to speak the truth about what you fear. Please think about some of the things about which you are afraid. Let your mind run as you complete as many of these sentences as possible:

    - I am afraid . . .

    - I am afraid . . .

    - I am afraid . . .

    - I am afraid . . .

    - I am afraid . . .

    - I am afraid . . .

    - I am afraid . . .

2. Many survivors feel terrible guilt or they feel deep shame and want to hide because they participated in something that felt wrong or that was forbidden. Please think about some of the things about which you feel guilt or shame. Let your mind run as you complete as many of these sentences as possible:

   - I feel guilty for . . .

   - If only . . .

   - I feel guilty for . . .

   - If only . . .

   - I feel shame about . . .

   - If only . . .

   - I feel shame about . . .

   - If only . . .

3. Guilt regarding the abuse is false guilt. True guilt is based on God's Word (p. 104). As you look at the list of things you feel guilty about, can you identify any guilt that is not based on the Word of God? Explain:

4. What hope do you have when you think about your guilt, both false and true, and understand that nothing is too big or too awful that the blood of Jesus cannot cover? Explain:

5. Anger is a normal response to abuse, evil, wrongdoing, and oppression. God responds to these things with anger, as well. However, anger that is not dealt with in healthy ways will go "sideways," and show up in destructive ways (p. 106). Think about your struggle with anger and check off the ways your anger has gone "sideways."

- ☐ I hurt other people
- ☐ I hurt myself
- ☐ I become emotionally flat, rather than risk expressing my anger
- ☐ I swallow my anger
- ☐ I have sudden outbursts or tantrums
- ☐ I become depressed
- ☐ I am afraid of my anger
- ☐ My anger is expressed through my body because I constantly struggle with headaches, stomach problems, and other painful or disruptive physical problems

6. Who have you been angry with regarding your abuse?

- ☐ My abuser(s)
- ☐ Silent or passive witnesses
- ☐ People in general
- ☐ Myself
- ☐ Church
- ☐ School
- ☐ Social Services

☐ Law Enforcement
☐ Other Organizations
☐
☐

7. Once abuse has occurred, the illusion that the world is "safe" is gone forever. To face your history means that you eventually must face your losses and grieve (p. 108). Do you fear grieving over your abuse? Explain:

8. As you think about your abuse, your childhood, your teen years, your life, what losses can you identify?

- I lost . . .

- I lost . . .

- I lost . . .

- I lost . . .

- I lost . . .

- I lost . . .

- I lost . . .

9. To grieve is to pass through the valley of the shadow of death (p. 109). You cannot do this alone. Take a few minutes and name a few safe people that you will allow to walk with you through this grieving process:

_____
_____
_____
_____
_____
_____
_____

10. Remember, while you are feeling grief over your losses, that you are not alone. Read Isaiah 61:1-3 and write down your ideas about how Jesus grieves with you:

11. Emotions are given to you by God, but abuse has damaged them. What emotions would you like to feel, that you have not experienced in a long time?

12. Write a prayer to Jesus and ask Him to give you the strength to push through the painful emotions so that you will eventually come out on the other side:

Chapter Fifteen–*Abuse Damaged Your Thinking*

Read Chapter Fifteen (pp. 111-118) and respond to the following questions, statements or projects:

1. Sexual abuse damaged your thinking. Often, we develop a way of thinking called *doublethink*. Please fill in the blanks (p. 112):

Doublethink is when we hold in our minds _____contradictory thoughts at the _____ time.

2. Are you aware of any ways that you doublethink? Explain:

3. As you identify ways that you doublethink, (p. 114) write statements to which you would respond, "Yes but . . .":

- _____!

    Yes, but _____.

- _____!

    Yes, but _____.

- _____!

    Yes, but _____.

- _____!

    Yes, but _____.

- _____!

    Yes, but _____.

4. Another way abuse damages some survivors of sexual abuse is called *dissociation*. Please fill in the blanks (p. 114):

Dissociation helps a survivor _____ physically or emotionally from the _____. You can dissociate from the _____ in your _____, from your _____, or from the _____ of what is happening.

5. Can you identify times when you have "spaced out" or "floated away?" Explain:

6. Can you identify what triggers the times you space out? Explain:

7. Why is dissociation so dangerous to an adult? Explain:

8. Abuse damages your memory and the ways your process your memories (p.115). As you think about your memories of abuse (what you remember, how you remember, what you do not remember, etc.) what confuses you and/or what does not confuse you? Complete these sentences:

 - I am confused by . . .

 - I am not confused by . . .

9. What does the statement "truth is more important than memories" mean to you?

10. To identify the *lies* and then replace them with **truth** is one of the major tasks you have in order to overcome damaged from sexual abuse (p. 117). How much energy have you devoted to maintaining the lie that the abuse did not happen or that it was no big deal? Explain:

11. Can you identify some of the twisted thinking and lies that you believe as the result of the abuse done to you? Explain:

12. What are some lies you have come to believe about yourself?

13. What are some lies you have come to believe about your relationships?

14. What are some lies you have come to believe about God?

15. What did your abuse teach you?

16. What do you think about the statement "healing will not come through maintaining . . . lies" (p. 118)? Explain:

17. Do you think that Jesus is afraid of your truth? Explain:

18. Write a prayer to Jesus about the struggles you have with the ways you think. Ask Him to give you the courage to have the lies you have believed exposed.

Chapter Sixteen–*Abuse Damaged Your Relationships*

Read Chapter Sixteen (pp. 119-128) and respond to the following questions, statements or projects:

1. Sexual abuse is something that occurs between two or more people. This means that it takes place in the context of relationships. On the check list below, identify the relationships you had with the people involved in your sexual abuse:

☐	Stranger	☐	Father's Girlfriend
☐	Mother	☐	Mentor
☐	Father	☐	Employer
☐	Uncle	☐	Church Worker
☐	Aunt	☐	Maintenance Worker
☐	Sister	☐	Doctor
☐	Brother	☐	Nurse
☐	Grandfather	☐	Counselor
☐	Grandmother	☐	Trafficker
☐	Teacher	☐	_____
☐	Pastor	☐	_____
☐	Scout Leader	☐	_____
☐	Sunday School Teacher	☐	_____
☐	Friend of the Family	☐	_____
☐	Neighbor		
☐	Sister's Friend		
☐	Brother's Friend		
☐	Babysitter		
☐	Brother-in-law		
☐	Sister-in-law		
☐	Step-mother		
☐	Step-father		
☐	Mother's Boyfriend		

2. When you think about how abuse has damaged your relationships (p. 121), which, if any, of these statements describe you:

   ☐ Relationships have been painful for me
   ☐ Relationships have been frightening for me
   ☐ Relationships have been chaotic for me
   ☐ I constantly look for better relationships because I have longings that are not being met
   ☐ I am disgusted with myself for having these longings
   ☐ I am so afraid of relationships that I try to avoid them
   ☐ Relationships make me feel as if I am in danger
   ☐ _____
   ☐ _____

3. The knowledge that you have about relationships, as a result of abuse, is based on lies which may have been repeated to you many times, with high emotional intensity (p. 122). Can you identify ways that you filter all of your incoming information about relationships through these lies? Explain:

4. *Trust* Trust is part of being in a relationship, and trust is damaged by abuse (p. 122). As you think about trust, check off what you have learned about trust:

   ☐ I act on what I trust to be true
   ☐ Some kinds of trust are risky and I am exposed to the potential of being hurt
   ☐ I trust in negative things
   ☐ Trust means to rely on integrity (being the same all the way through)
   ☐ I learned to trust people to be one thing, when all evidence indicated that they were not trust worthy
   ☐ I see every relationship through the eyes of abuse

☐ Even when there are warning bells going off in my head about a person, I still trust them and end up in another abusive relationship

5. What are your patterns of trust or distrust in relationships? Explain:

6. Do you trust anyone? Explain why:

7. How do you decide whether or not to trust someone?

8. What do you do if a person fails to prove trustworthy?

9. What can other people trust that they will get from you?

10. Does trusting frighten you, or do you do it blindly? Explain:

11. Do you ever try to control others so you can guarantee a safe outcome for yourself in the relationship? Explain:

12. **<u>Boundaries</u>** Sexual abuse is a gross violation of boundaries (p. 125). Identify ways that your boundaries were violated as a result of abuse:

13. When your abuser(s) took what should have been asked for and then refused to give you what you needed, you felt violated and confused about boundaries (p. 126). Identify ways that you have struggled with boundaries in your life:

- ☐ I do not realize that I have the right to say "no"
- ☐ I frequently let people do what they want to me, without expressing my needs or desires
- ☐ I am unable to draw lines, and frequently find myself in the position of being a victim
- ☐ I protect my boundaries like a vicious guard dog
- ☐ I never rest because I am so diligent about protecting myself
- ☐ I have trouble believing that I do not have to give whatever anyone wants from me
- ☐ I frequently feel as if I have no voice and no choice
- ☐ I have trouble setting limits

☐ All of my choices about relationship boundaries are based on fear
☐
☐
☐
☐

14. <u>*Control*</u>. Sexual abuse often leads survivors to a very high need to control relationships (p. 128). Identify ways that you try control others:

15. Do you feel able to maintain healthy relationship boundaries? Explain:

16. Do you exercise your voice effectively in relationships? Explain:

Chapter Seventeen–*Abuse Damaged Your Spirit*

Read Chapter Seventeen (pp. 129-135) and respond to the following questions, statements or projects:

1. Sexual abuse deeply touches your spirit and hinders your ability to hope (p. 129). Read the paragraph on page 131 about "Mister Jesus." and write your thoughts and feelings about what you read:

2. After reading the "Mister Jesus" paragraph on page 131, identify how this affects where you are with God:

3. Children learn about the "unseen" by what they "see" (p. 132). When you think about your abuse (what was "seen"), what did you learn about the "unseen?" Explain:

4. Trauma stops growth (p. 133). Have you heard and believed truths about God, but feel as if your spirit is frozen and unable to really feel God? Describe what you feel and think:

5. Sexual abuse creates a "disorder of hope" (p. 134). Have you experienced life without hope? Explain:

6. Have you brought God's character into question because of your sexual abuse? Explain:

7. When you think about the evil of abuse and the goodness of God, what ideas do you have about God? Explain:

8. Do you believe that God can stand up to your hard questions about His character and the abuse that was done to you? Explain:

PART FOUR–WHAT DOES HEALING LOOK LIKE?
Chapter 18–22 (pp. 137–187)

Chapter Eighteen–*Healing for Your Body*

Read Chapter Eighteen (pp. 139-147) and respond to the following questions, statements or projects:

1. Healing will come for your body (p. 139) by reconnecting with your body and learning to think about it differently. Have you felt disconnected from your body? Explain:

2. Have you been unable to respond appropriately to your body because you do not feel anything? Explain:

3. Have you abused substances in order not to feel? Explain:

4. As an exercise to reconnect with your body, sit outside and face the sun and answer these questions:

- What does the sun feel like on your body?

- What do you like about what you feel physically?

- What don't you like about what you feel physically?

5. Choose another activity, such as walking in the rain, that will give you a chance to record your responses. What activity have you chosen?

6. Now, answer these questions about the activity you have chosen:

- What does it feel like on your body?

- What do you like about what you feel physically?

- What don't you like about what you feel physically?

7. What do you think might happen when you begin to physically feel what you have physically ignored? Explain:

8. What have your past coping mechanisms been when your body has felt something that reminds you of your abuse (p. 141)? Explain:

9. As you think about healing for your body, think about how will you re-direct your responses when your body feels something that reminds you of your abuse (p. 142)? Think about a specific new response that you can use instead of this old coping mechanism (such as writing in a journal instead of drinking alcohol). Identify this new response and explain how you will use it:

10. You have the power to choose what to do with your body (p. 142). How do you think you will be able to glorify God with your body? Explain:

11. What do you think it was like for Jesus to live in a body? Explain:

12. Does the fact that Jesus lived in a body have anything to do with how you will live in yours? Explain:

13. Read Romans 12:1. Whose character is revealed in your body? Your abuser's character? Christ's character? A victim's character? Explain:

14. When you know Christ as the Savior, then His Spirit lives in your body. Because of this, how will you care for your body, protect it from evil, and maintain its integrity? Explain:

Chapter Nineteen–*Healing for Your Emotions*

Read Chapter Nineteen (pp. 149-158) and respond to the following questions, statements or projects:

1. Sexual abuse traumatizes people, and fear is the core response to trauma (p. 151). In order to heal from the trauma, you must identify the fear. Think about your fears and write them here:

2. Is it difficult for you to find words to express your fears?

3. If words are difficult for you, select some other ways to express your fears (p. 152). This will help you to recover your voice. Listed below are other ways to express your fears. Place a check next to the ones that you might want to try:
    - ☐ Make a collage
    - ☐ Use words of other survivors
    - ☐ Paint
    - ☐ Draw
    - ☐ Sculpt with clay
    - ☐ Dance
    - ☐ Find music that expresses what you fear
    - ☐ Write music
    - ☐ Sing
    - ☐ _____
    - ☐ _____

4. Trauma from abuse shuts up most survivors and they find themselves "stuck" in fear (p. 152). Identify ways that your fears keep showing up in your life (such as flashbacks):

5. How do you think giving voice to your experiences will help you to separate the truth from the lies? Explain:

6. Why do you think that dealing with your damaged emotions will require hard work and repetition in order to find healing? Explain:

7. Jesus felt fear in the Garden of Gethsemane the night before He was crucified (p. 155). In what ways can you identify with the fear He experienced? Explain:

8. Jesus was treated as if He was guilty, when He was not (p. 156). In what ways can you identify with this? Explain:

9. Jesus became a guilt offering so that you could be free from guilt (p. 156). Where you are truly guilty, Jesus has made a way for you to be free. What does this idea mean to you? Explain:

10. Jesus was despised and one from whom people hid their faces. How do you identify with this sense of shame? Explain:

11. Jesus got angry over anything that dishonored or misrepresented God. Jesus is angry about abuse because it is evil, it is sin, it has damaged you. Have you been angry at abuse and the abuse of others? Have you been angry because of the lies you were told about yourself and God? Explain:

12. The danger of anger is that it is a fast-moving emotion that rises up and out very quickly (p. 157). This makes it easy for you to let your anger take over and magnify your sinful, self-centered ways. Identify ways that your anger has not reflected the pure anger of Jesus:

13. Read Isaiah 53:4. What has Jesus done with your grief? Explain:

14. Think about the emotional suffering of Jesus. How will meditating on His emotional suffering draw you closer to Jesus for understanding, comfort and healing? Explain:

Chapter Twenty–*Healing for Your Thinking*

Read Chapter Twenty (pp. 159-166) and respond to the following questions, statements or projects:

1. Sexual abuse damages your thinking. Healing comes through replacing the lies with truth (p. 159). There are both good and bad realities that are simultaneously true (p.162). Place a check mark next to the realities that you know are true:

Bad Realities

- ☐ There are evil people in the world
- ☐ The world is full of lies and deceit
- ☐ People will do terrible violence to others to gratify something twisted in themselves.
- ☐ There is darkness, chaos, and trash in the world
- ☐ Sorrow can be crushing
- ☐ Grief can be intense
- ☐ Rage can be uncontrolled
- ☐ Fear can be overwhelming
- ☐ I am not always in control
- ☐ I cannot always protect myself
- ☐ I cannot always protect people I love
- ☐ I am capable of hurting others
- ☐ I am capable of lies and deceit

Good Realities

- ☐ Beauty exists
- ☐ Love exists
- ☐ I have seen love in action
- ☐ Trust exists
- ☐ I know people who speak truth
- ☐ I know that there is light in this dark world
- ☐ God exists

- ☐ God is truth, love and beauty
- ☐ Jesus Christ revealed God's character
- ☐ Jesus Christ has felt what I feel

2. Look up 1 John 5:19-20 and write out these verses:

3. 1 John 5:19-20 truthfully explains the world we live in (p. 163). According to this Scripture, what is the whole truth about the world (the power of the evil one vs. the power of Jesus)? Explain:

4. Because of the work of the evil one in your life you need healing, love, someone to carry your grief, and comfort (p. 164). God knows how to break free from the evil one's damage. Check the truths below you need God to use to help you break free:

    - ☐ The evil one has no authority over Jesus
    - ☐ The power of the evil one will come to an end at the appointed time
    - ☐ Jesus came to give me life
    - ☐ Jesus came to be my healer
    - ☐ Jesus is the lover of my soul
    - ☐ Jesus is my burden bearer
    - ☐ Jesus sent me a Comforter (the Holy Spirit)
    - ☐ The Comforter will guide me so that I may know God
    - ☐ The more I seek God, the more I am changed to be like Him

5. Make two lists, below. On one, list the things you know about the power of the evil one that FIT with God's TRUTH. On the other, list the things you know about the Son of God that are TRUE (p. 164):

Here is what I know about the power of the evil one that fits with God's TRUTH:	*Here is what I know about the Son of God that fits with God's TRUTH:*
▪	▪
▪	▪
▪	▪
▪	▪
▪	▪
▪	▪
▪	

6. Healing comes for your damaged thinking patterns when you begin to replace the lies with the truth (p. 159). Jesus lived in a body like yours and put Himself in the middle of the battle between lies and truth (p. 165). Place a check mark next to what is true about Jesus:

- ☐ Jesus lived in a human body
- ☐ Jesus felt emotions like mine
- ☐ Jesus waged war with the father of lies
- ☐ Jesus knows what it is like to fight lies and deceit
- ☐ Jesus knows the strength of some lies
- ☐ Jesus fought the liar so that I could live in truth
- ☐ Jesus met evil people just like I did.
- ☐ Jesus experienced violence because of the twisted demands of some people just like I did.

- ☐ Jesus experienced darkness, chaos and trash just like I did
- ☐ Jesus actually went down to hell itself to fight for my right to truth
- ☐ Jesus knows what it is like to have bad things happen and not be in control just like I did
- ☐ Jesus knows what it is like to be unprotected just like I did
- ☐ Jesus knows what it is like not to get what He needed just like I did
- ☐ Jesus experienced terrible pain just like I have
- ☐ Jesus understands me
- ☐ Jesus can help me untangle the lies from the truth

7. When you begin to take the lies you have believed, and hold them up to the truth of Jesus, you can begin to see the lies for the evil that they are. When the truth of Jesus begins to replace the lies of the evil one, then the way you live will begin to change (p. 166). Write a prayer to Jesus about how you need Him to help you with your struggles to live in truth:

Chapter Twenty-One–*Healing for Your Relationships*

Read Chapter Twenty-One (pp. 167-176) and respond to the following questions, statements or projects:

1. Sexual abuse damages your relationships. The lies and confusion spill over into other relationships (p. 168). Take a few minutes to list the names of a few people that are important relationships to you at this time:

Name (example: Mary)	Relationship to You (example: wife)

2. When you think about these relationships, please check off the ways that the lies and confusion from your abuse have harmed your relationships (p. 168):

- ☐ I have isolated myself even though I long for intimacy
- ☐ Since trust was broken, I am careful to guard myself and protect myself
- ☐ Limits and boundaries make little sense to me
- ☐ I intrude too much and people get angry or annoyed with me
- ☐ I over-commit because I do not understand that limits are normal
- ☐ I have a hard time believing that it is okay to say "no"
- ☐ I want love but I put a wall between me and people who love me
- ☐ When relationships get complicated, I want to give up
- ☐ _____
- ☐ _____
- ☐ _____

3. One key to having healthy relationships is to understand what is realistic to expect. Unhealthy relationships usually mean that you (1) expect nothing or that you (2) think what you are getting is in your relationships is all wrong (p. 169). Please check off ways that you have had unrealistic expectations in your relationships:

    - ☐ I don't expect anything from anyone
    - ☐ I never open my mouth to express myself
    - ☐ I never ask for anything
    - ☐ I work hard to figure out what other people want and then give it to them so that I won't get hurt
    - ☐ I don't believe that what I think, want or need matters to other people
    - ☐ I seem to be taken advantage of quite a bit
    - ☐ Nobody gives me what I want or need
    - ☐ I keep getting confused about what I want from people and I should expect from them that is reasonable
    - ☐ I panic when what I long for does not happen, then I overreact and trash the relationship
    - ☐ _____
    - ☐ _____
    - ☐ _____

4. Sexual abuse means that most of your relationships are based on fear. One way to begin healing for your relationships is to learn to respond to people out of love rather than fear. Read the second paragraph on page 171 and complete the following phrases:

    - Fear guards; love _____.
    - Fear hides; love _____.
    - Fear shuts up: love _____.
    - Fear panics; love _____.
    - Fear keeps a record; love _____ graciously.

5. Read 1 John 4:18 and complete the following sentences: "There is no _____ in _____. But perfect _____ drives out _____, because fear has to do with _____. The one who _____ is not made perfect in _____."

6. Fear causes you to punish other people (p. 172). Please check off ways that you have punished people because of fear:
   ☐ I seek revenge when someone has done what I was afraid they would do
   ☐ I act hateful to people
   ☐ I withhold myself from people
   ☐ I withdraw from people
   ☐ I fail to speak truth
   ☐ I do not act out of love
   ☐ I am afraid I will be hurt
   ☐ I am afraid people will not give me enough
   ☐ I am afraid I will not get enough attention
   ☐ I am afraid I will not get enough love
   ☐ I constantly measure people and keep score
   ☐ I make sure I keep who I am hidden
   ☐ I wonder if people will discover who I am and reject me
   ☐ I am never at rest in relationship

7. Read 1 John 2:10-11. If you hate, resent or fear people, you invite darkness into your life. Fear blinds you, and confuses your thinking. If you want to see clearly, you must love. How do you think godly love will help you to see clearly and help you to think clearly?

8. Forgiveness is about having fellowship with God (p. 174). How do you think forgiveness will free you from destructive thoughts and emotions? Explain:

9. Take a look at the table you made of your relationships (earlier in this project) and transfer their names and relationships to the table below. Now, identify ways that you have responded to these people out of fear rather than love (be specific). Then think about ways you could shift from fear to love and write your ideas (be specific):

Name	Relationship to You	Ways that I have responded to him/her out of fear	Ways that I could respond to him/her in love
Example: Mary	Ex: Wife	Ex: I have to know where she is every minute of every day because I am afraid I will lose her or that she will throw me away. I have accused her of not loving me when she gets frustrated with me.	Ex: I need to recognize that she is her own person and trust her regardless of the unreasonable fear I have of losing her. I need to respect her needs to express her true feelings and listen to her frustrations rather than to my panic of being rejected.

10. Jesus lived in relationships with people just like you do. He also lived in a relationship with God just like you do (p.174). Write down your ideas about the following questions:
    - What were the relationships like for the One who was perfect love? Explain:

- Did Jesus experience rejection? Explain:

- Did Jesus experience betrayal? Explain:

- Did Jesus experience abandonment? Explain:

- Does Jesus know the depth of your relational pain? Explain:

11. Read 1 Peter 5:7. In what ways do you think Jesus can help you respond to your relationships in love instead of fear? Explain:

Chapter Twenty-Two–*Healing for Your Spirit*

Read Chapter Twenty-Two (pp. 177-187) and respond to the following questions, statements or projects:

1. Healing comes through learning the character of God as it is revealed in Jesus Christ (p. 177). What do you know about God's character from Jesus' teachings and how He lived on earth?

2. People work hard to understand things (p. 179). Is it possible for you to understand everything? Explain:

3. Read Isaiah 45:3. What promise has God made to you in this verse? (p. 180)

4. This world, for right now, remains in the power of the evil one (p. 180). What are some of the lies that Satan wants you to believe about God?

5. When you are in pain, you need people to "get it." Do you think Jesus understands your pain? Explain:

6. On your healing journey, you will need to re-arrange the questions and ask "Who are You, God?" Then you ask the next question, "Why?" With the questions re-arranged in this order, where do you need to go to find Jesus (p. 181)?

7. Read the following Scriptures and write down what God reveals to you about <u>WHO</u> He is and how He relates to your suffering:
- Psalm 10

- Psalm 22

- Psalm 86

- Psalm 88

8. Read Isaiah 53 and then read the comments recorded on p. 182-185. What are your thoughts about Who God is and how He relates to your abuse?

9. Identify ways that you will listen to God:

10. How is Jesus your "treasure" in the darkness? Explain:

PART FIVE–FINDING OTHERS TO HELP

Read Chapters Twenty-Two through Twenty-Five (pp. 189-213) and answer the following question (based on Chapter Twenty-Five (pp. 207-213):

1. After reading Chapter Twenty-Five, what does "home" mean to you?

2. What do you think the Holy Spirit is saying to you at this time?

CPSIA information can be obtained at www.ICGtesting.com
Printed in the USA
LVOW09s1749270314

379220LV00007B/1115/P

9 781628 716078